2. Magnificent bird of paradise

The magnificent bird of paradise has a harsh call, almost like a raven or crow. But this changes to high-pitched notes when it is trying to attract a mate!

6. King bird of paradise

This bird loudly calls for a mate, spreading his wings in a courtship display.

5. Lesser bird of paradise

The high-pitched repeated screech you can hear is the voice of the lesser bird of paradise.

PRESS HERE ♪

Birds of the Mountains

It's hard to believe that any birds can survive up in the Himalayan Mountains, 16,000 feet above sea level. However, if you listen closely, you can hear calls through the sound of the wind whistling through the peaks. Geese and cranes are making their yearly migrations, calling on their way, while another bird watches silently as they go by . . .

5. Lammergeier

This "bearded" vulture has a high-pitched screech. It's known for smashing bones onto rocks and eating the marrow inside.

4. Red-billed chough

The red-billed chough is a kind of crow. It makes a short call as it performs spectacular aerobatic flights.

1. Raven

The distinctive, deep-throated caw you can hear belongs to the common raven, the biggest member of the crow family.

2. Himalayan snowcock

The long, high-pitched sound is the Himalayan snowcock's. Its gray-and-white plumage camouflages itself against the brown-and-white rocks and snow.

PRESS HERE ♪

6. Bar-headed goose

The bar-headed geese honk loudly as they make their trip. They are the world's highest flying bird, soaring to over 20,000 feet!

7. Golden eagle

This golden eagle is hoping to hunt a demoiselle crane so it makes no sound at all—the success of its mission relies on it being as silent as possible.

3. Demoiselle crane

Each demoiselle crane has a range of different calls, which it uses to talk with the flock when migrating. Sometimes distress calls are used to alert others to threats, like golden eagles!

Birds of the Desert

In the Sonoran desert in the USA, dry, barren sand lands stretch as far as the eye can see, with few cacti or even shrubs to provide shelter. The first thing you hear is the rattlesnake, who hopes to scare off an unlikely attacker with its harsh rattle. As you listen and watch more closely, you notice the skies are almost bare . . . here, most birds prefer to run than fly!

4. Black-throated sparrow

Locally, this bird is also called the desert sparrow because it likes to live in hot, dry climates, where few other birds are found. Flocks make tinkling calls while foraging on the ground in open areas.

2. Le Conte's thrasher

The pale feathers of this songbird blend in with the sands of the desert, helping it to avoid predators. It runs around fast with its tail cocked up above its back, looking for bugs and small animals to eat. When it perches, often in a saltbush, you will hear its warbled song.

5. Gambel's quail

These noisy, sociable birds call to each other as they run to safety, or stage a lookout in low bushes.

PRESS HERE ♪

3. Gilded flicker

The gilded flicker is a large woodpecker that has a canny way of protecting its young: it digs a nest in a saguaro cactus, and lays its white eggs there.

1. Greater roadrunner

Unlike most birds, the greater roadrunner prefers to walk or run, and will fly only when absolutely necessary. The clackety sound you can hear is an alarm call, as this bird battles something most birds would steer well clear of . . . a rattlesnake!

Birds of the Prairie

Once, vast areas of grassland covered North America. There is too little rain for trees to grow here, but grass is able to reach 3 feet below the surface, anchoring the soil in storms. Now, only small areas of true prairie remain, but listen closely and you'll hear that these lands are still alive with the sound of insects buzzing, grouse drumming, and songbirds twittering.

1. Greater prairie chicken

During mating season, males make low, booming calls that can be heard over a mile away. Because so much of their habitat has disappeared, these birds are at risk of becoming extinct, and the spooky sound means they are now called "the ghosts of the grasslands."

7. Dickcissel

The dickcissel is named for its call, which sounds like, "dick-dick-cissel." It spends most of its time close to the earth, nesting on the ground and feeding on seeds, spiders, grasshoppers, and crickets. Nearly all dickcissels make long distance migrations during the winter.

4. Bobolink

A small songbird, the bobolink can be seen singing away on a grass stem, or flying low over the grass. Some people think they look like they're wearing a tuxedo back to front!

3. Burrowing owl

Instead of roosting in trees, this tiny owl lives in burrows underground, either dug themselves or taken over from another animal. It makes a low pitched "twoo-twoo" sound.

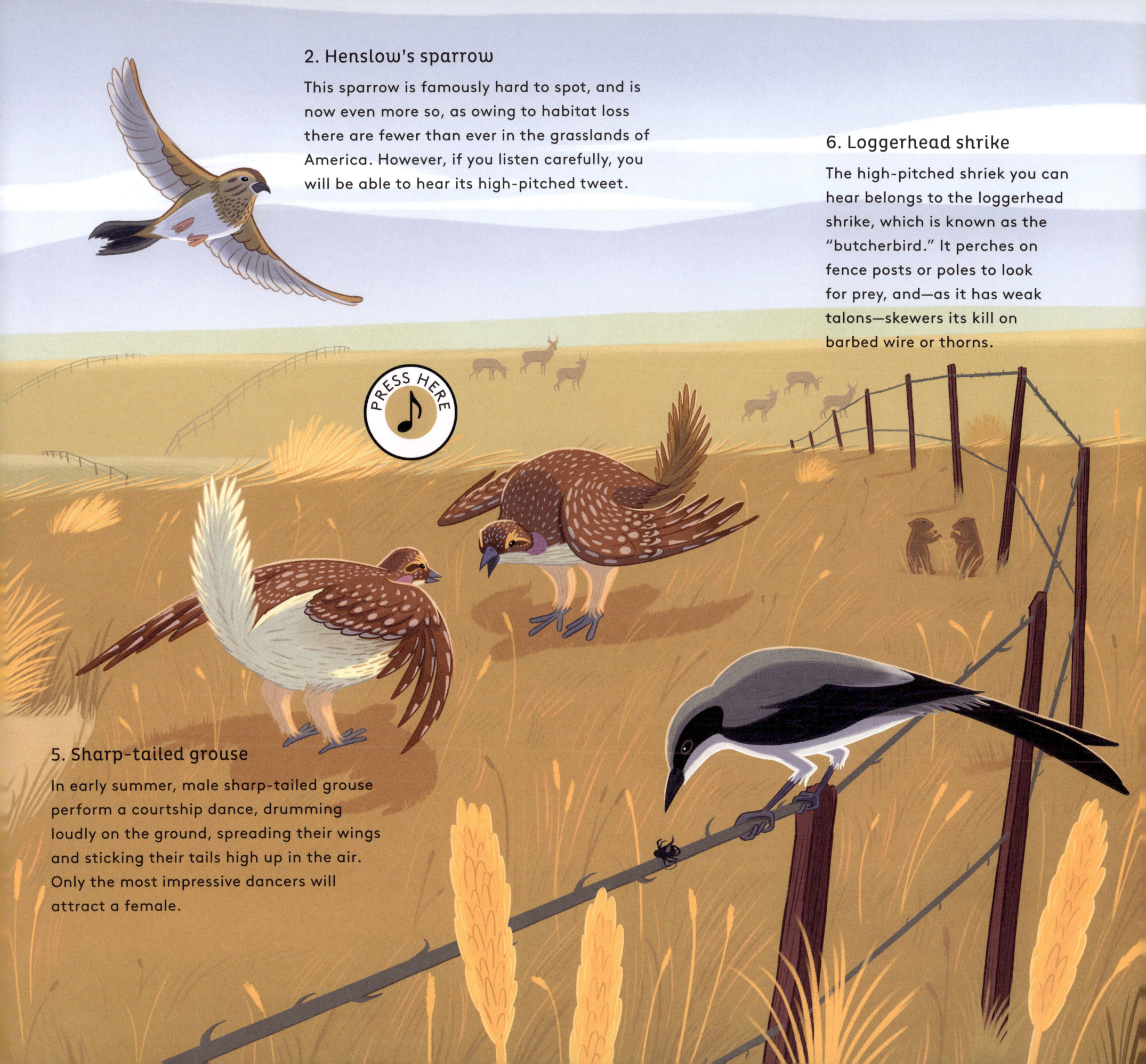

2. Henslow's sparrow

This sparrow is famously hard to spot, and is now even more so, as owing to habitat loss there are fewer than ever in the grasslands of America. However, if you listen carefully, you will be able to hear its high-pitched tweet.

6. Loggerhead shrike

The high-pitched shriek you can hear belongs to the loggerhead shrike, which is known as the "butcherbird." It perches on fence posts or poles to look for prey, and—as it has weak talons—skewers its kill on barbed wire or thorns.

PRESS HERE ♪

5. Sharp-tailed grouse

In early summer, male sharp-tailed grouse perform a courtship dance, drumming loudly on the ground, spreading their wings and sticking their tails high up in the air. Only the most impressive dancers will attract a female.

Birds of the Woods

It's early morning deep in an English forest, and songbirds chirp to announce the arrival of the dawn. Spring is here, and many birds have returned, flying thousands of miles from warmer lands. They are here to breed, so they're singing their hearts out to find a mate, or taking care of their nests. However, they must always be on the lookout . . . birds of prey and other predators like foxes live here too.

4. Wood warbler

These small green birds sing from high-up in the forest canopy, but actually build their nests on the ground in hollows. Their scientific name "sibilatrix" means "the whistler."

2. Greater spotted woodpecker

The drumming sound you can hear is made by this woodpecker. It makes this sound to tell other birds that this tree is his territory, to uncover small insects or to drill holes to nest.

6. Goldfinch

The long, pointed beak of the goldfinch is specialized for getting seeds out of thistles and other plants. This noisy bird gathers in small flocks and has a twittering call.

1. Blackbird

Confusingly, it's only male blackbirds that are black with a distinctive orange eye ring. The females are brown. The beautiful song of blackbirds is heard in many woods in Europe. You'll most often see them pecking for bugs and worms at the bottom of hedges or shrubs.

7. Cuckoo

The cuckoo flies to Africa or Southeast Asia for the winter, so its unmistakable "cuckoo-cuckoo" sound is one of the distinctive sounds of spring! Cuckoos lay their eggs in the nests of other birds rather than building their own.

5. Tawny owl

About the size of a pigeon, at night the tawny owl can be heard making a "twit-twoo" sound when it is courting. It perches in the trees, dropping down on prey like voles and mice.

3. Kingfisher

A flash of blue in the forest, the kingfisher makes a high-pitched call on its way to the river to hunt. It eats mostly small fish, which it dives into the water to grab, then whacks against a tree to stun or kill.

PRESS HERE ♪

Birds of the Ice

The bottom of the world in breeding season is a noisy place! Colonies of penguins hold chicks that chatter and gabble, while high in the air, skuas, albatrosses, and petrels call as they scan the surface for prey. Smaller birds better watch out, as in this icy world, everyone is on the lookout for food.

4. Antarctic tern

Antarctic terns fish in flocks of up to several hundred birds. After their eggs have hatched they have to defend their chicks for several weeks from hungry skuas and kelp gulls. This short "kip-kip" cry is used to sound the alarm.

2. Wilson's storm petrel

That scratchy sound you can hear belongs to the storm petrel, one of the most common seabird species in the world. It feeds by running close to the sea's surface, dropping its head down to scoop up food like fish and squid.

5. Adélie penguin

Adélie penguins are smaller than emperor penguins, with a scratchier call. They are excellent swimmers and will often dive into the water with a splash.

6. Dominican gull

The distinctive seagull call belongs to the Dominican gull, which was named after the Dominican order of friars who wear black-and-white habits. They eat whatever they can get their hands on—sometimes even their own eggs and chicks!

7. Wandering albatross

This albatross holds the record for the bird with the largest wingspan, measuring a whopping 11 feet! These huge wings let them glide for hours without resting or even flapping. They make whistles, grunts, and even screams like this.

3. Brown skua

This bird is the one all the others keep a lookout for, as it will prey on other seabirds and their young, as well as eggs, fish, mollusks, and even small mammals. It uses scratchy calls to sound the alarm or talk to other skuas.

1. Emperor penguin

The constant chattering sound of emperor penguin chicks, and the longer answering calls from their parents, tells you that you're in the Antarctic. As the chicks get bigger, adults leave more and more often to find food in the sea, which they will swallow and then drop into their offspring's mouths when they return.

PRESS HERE ♪

Birds of the Wetlands

In Lake Nakuru in Kenya, huge flocks of flamingos turn the water pink. Up to 2 million flamingos gather here, making this one of the most incredible bird spectacles on the planet! However, these wetlands are home to other birds too. Pelicans gobble fish using their huge bills, eagles and storks fight over food, and if you listen carefully, you'll be able to hear the booming call of the biggest bird of all . . .

1. Flamingo

Both lesser and greater flamingos chatter and squeal at Lake Nakuru. The lesser species feeds mostly on algae. Their droppings in turn make more algae grow, creating food for them in the future. Greater flamingos are bigger than lesser, standing at 4 feet tall, and feed on small fish and plankton as well as algae.

7. African fish eagle

African fish eagles call to other birds to let them know that this is their territory. Males have higher-pitched calls than females. They get their name from the way they dive to the water's surface to catch fish from their talons.

3. Marabou stork

This large bird will often fight with the African fish eagle over prey, which includes flamingos. It has long legs, ideal for wading through water. The low-pitched call it makes sounds almost like a cow mooing.

5. Gray heron

The gray heron hunts very differently to the pelican. It stands totally still and silent in the water on its long legs, waiting for a fish to swim near so it can pounce. When it's flying, it makes harsh, cough-like calls to others.

6. Ostrich

The biggest bird of all lives in the dry grasses and deserts of Africa, but it can sometimes be spotted by lakes. It uses its powerful kick to see off any animal that gets too close. The low booming sound you can hear is made by the ostrich inflating its neck.

4. Great-white pelican

You'll most often see this bird preening and bathing, as its feeding is normally done by 9am each day! Pelicans feed in groups, communicating in low grunts, forcing fish into shallow water and then scooping them up in their large, elastic bills.

PRESS HERE ♪

2. Yellow-billed duck

The distinctive "quack-quack" you can hear belongs to a female yellow-billed duck. This water bird feeds mainly on plants, but sometimes insects and shellfish too.

Birds of the City

In early-evening Paris, a flock of chattering starlings swoop and dive against the darkening sky. Pigeons coo, flapping away in alarm when cyclists approach. The city is full of birds that have cleverly adapted to make these streets their home, from magpies using tools to find food to the sharp-eyed peregrine falcon, swooping from high buildings to find its prey . . .

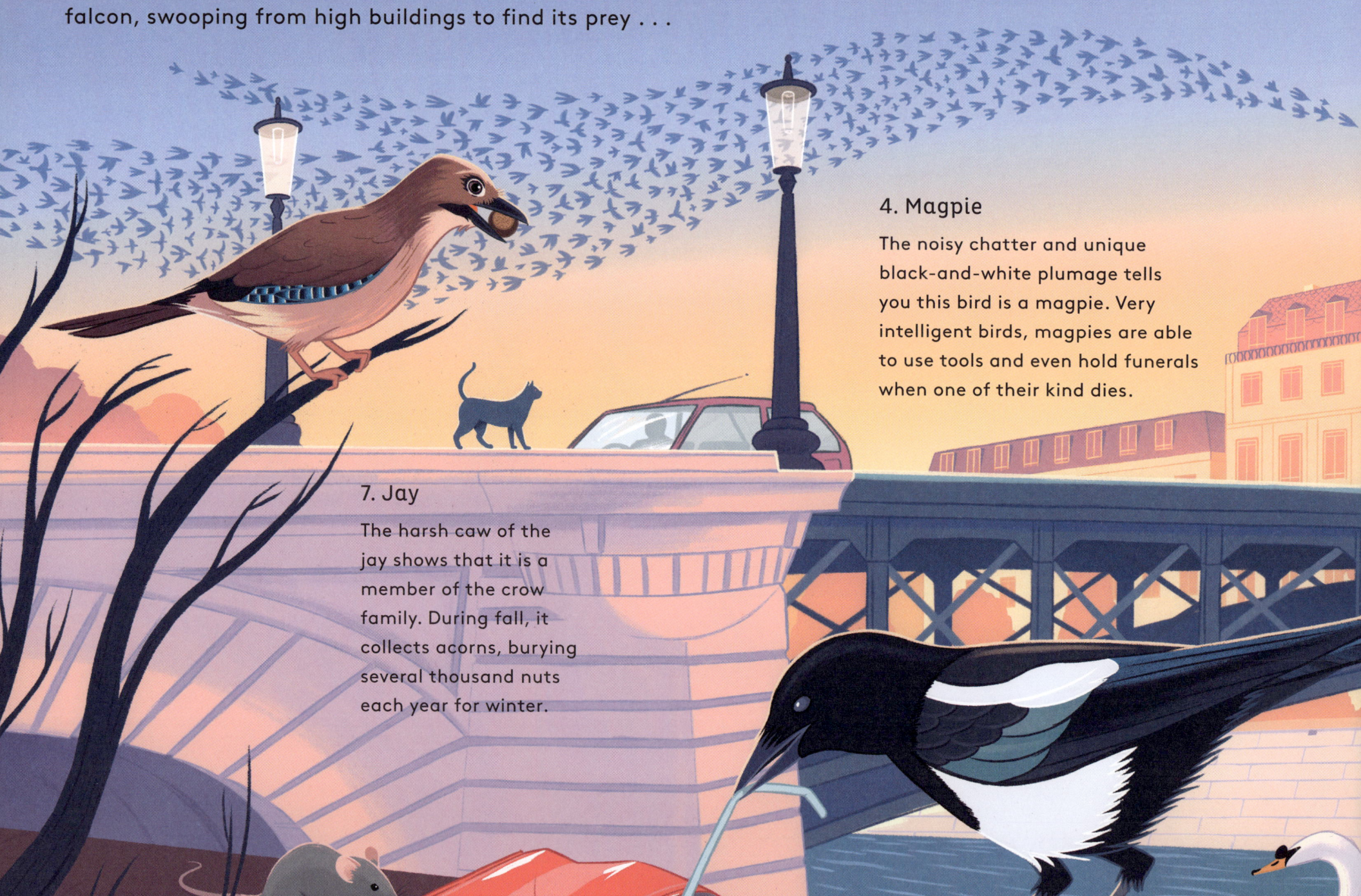

5. Starling

The chirpy starling can nest in trees, buildings, and rooftops, so it's a common site in cities. At dusk, starlings gather in huge flocks and perform incredible flying displays.

4. Magpie

The noisy chatter and unique black-and-white plumage tells you this bird is a magpie. Very intelligent birds, magpies are able to use tools and even hold funerals when one of their kind dies.

7. Jay

The harsh caw of the jay shows that it is a member of the crow family. During fall, it collects acorns, burying several thousand nuts each year for winter.

6. Domestic pigeon

You can tell from their cooing sound that pigeons are descended from wild rock doves, which nest in cliff crevices. In cities, they nest in tall buildings instead. They eat whatever is on offer, including thrown-away bagels, popcorn, and cake!

2. Peregrine falcon

The screeching call you can hear belongs to the peregrine falcon, an aerial predator that is increasingly making high buildings in the city its home.

PRESS HERE

3. Mute swan

This beautiful species has a squeaky honking call, and holds its long neck in a graceful curve. Large and sometimes aggressive, it's best to keep your distance if you see a swan in a city park or river!

1. Blue tit

A common garden bird, the blue tit eats insects, seeds, and nuts, and in some countries has been known to follow milkmen around, taking sips from milk bottles by piercing through the foil tops. Their bright feathers and high-pitched song makes them easy to recognize.

Birds of the Ocean

Some ocean birds spend most of their lives at sea, returning to land only to breed, while others prefer to stay near the coast. Either way, these incredible birds have adapted to their ocean lifestyles. They feed mainly on fish, some of them have salt glands to handle all the saltwater they drink while feeding, and they have webbed feet to help them move through water. These adaptations are crucial for survival in this watery world.

2. Cory's shearwater

The Cory's shearwater is well adapted to living at sea, with long, narrow wings and feet placed far back on its body to help it swim better. Some people call it the "wacka wacka" bird because of the noise it makes!

3. White-breasted cormorant

This bird has a low, croaky sound. When nesting in colonies, to get their supper, cormorants dive to depths of 30 feet, grabbing fish in their beaks. Back on land, they stretch their wings out to dry their feathers!

6. Cape gannet

This flock of large gannets call as they're drawn into a feeding frenzy—a shoal of sardines is being attacked from both above and below! Good divers and swimmers, the gannets hit the ocean's surface at up to 75 miles per hour.

1. Common tern

These seabirds occur off the shores of Africa in flocks of thousands, making sharp screeching sounds. They breed in Europe, but when it gets too cold in the winter they migrate thousands of miles to Africa.

7. Black-browed albatross

The black-browed albatross is medium-sized, with a wingspan of over 6 feet. They fly low to the surface of the ocean, eating krill, fish, and sometimes even jellyfish, and bray to mark their territory.

4. African oystercatcher

The high shriek belongs to this black bird, which got its name because of its liking for shellfish. It feeds mainly on mussels and limpets, prying shells open with its long beak.

5. African penguin

Unlike their Antarctic cousins, African penguins don't need to worry about the cold! They have a loud, wheezing call which sounds a bit like a donkey, giving them the nickname "jackass penguin." They breed in colonies and feed on small fish.

PRESS HERE ♪

Birds of the Bush

Very few people live in the Australian outback. Animals and birds must live off the land, taking what they can in conditions that are often hot and harsh. However, because they have been left alone, many species have flourished here. If you're brave enough to venture to this land of explorers and dreams, you'll discover a whole world, with sights and sounds that might surprise you!

1. Sulphur-crested cockatoo

The sound you'll most often hear from these noisy parrots is a harsh screech, used when flying, perching, or to sound the alarm. Friendly and sociable, cockatoos gather in flocks to forage either on the ground or in trees for seeds.

2. Tawny frogmouth

The tawny frogmouth looks a bit like a cross between an owl and a frog, and is named because of the huge frog-like bite which is used to eat insects. It mainly communicates in short, low-pitched throbbing sounds.

5. Major Mitchell's cockatoo

This small pink-and-white parrot was named after Major Mitchell, one of the first European explorers of inland Australia. It talks to others in a high, quavering call.

PRESS HERE ♪

4. Superb fairy-wren

The chirping song you can hear is the superb fairy wren, and its brown plumage shows that it's a female. Males have bright blue heads, chests, and tail feathers.

6. Emu

Watch out—the biggest bird in the outback has arrived! Emus can grow up to 6 feet and are second only to ostriches in height. Their low grunting sound is like that of a cassowary, and sure enough, they're from the same family.

7. Laughing kookaburra

What's that loud cackling sound? It's the distinctive song of the laughing kookaburra, a large kingfisher. If a rival tribe threatens, a whole family of kookaburras will gather to warn them off with their cackles.

3. Zebra finch

This Australian finch has a short, thick, pointed red bill for eating seeds. Each male zebra finch learns how to sing by imitating others, but will end up with a personal song that's totally unique.

What are birds?

Birds are a type of animal that has cleverly adapted for flight. Its main wing bone is hollow, which means it has a lighter body that is easier to carry in the air. Its wings are carefully shaped to help the bird fly, with feathers that are shaped into points. In fact, airplane wings are modeled after bird wings!

Although birds are known for their ability to fly, some also can run, swim, dive, and jump. And some birds, like penguins, don't fly, but still have wings. Many birds have sharp beaks which they use to grab food. So that they don't have to carry extra weight in flight, birds give birth to their young by laying eggs. They must keep these warm during incubation, as birds are warm-blooded. Fossil records show us that these amazing animals evolved alongside the dinosaurs during the Jurassic Period, 160 million years ago. Birds are in fact the closest relatives of dinosaurs that walk the Earth today.

There are many different types of birds, grouped together into orders and families depending on their features. Here are some of the most common orders. Can you find them in this book?

- Passeriformes

This is the largest order, which includes more than half of all bird species. Passerines are known as perching birds, and include wrens, warblers, tits, birds of paradise, and finches.

- Columbidae

Columbines are pigeons and doves and are amongst the most common birds in the world.

- Strigiformes

These birds have a large head, sharp talons, good vision, and feathers that have adapted to be as silent as possible. That's right, they're owls!

- Anseriformes

This order of waterbirds includes duck, geese, and swans.

- Procellariiformes

These seabirds include albatrosses, petrels, and shearwaters.

The sounds in this book were created in association with The Macaulay Library at the Cornell Lab of Ornithology Emu recording © Marc Anderson, XC233818. Accessible at www.xeno-canto.org/233818